Read Up Jot Down™ Journaling Series

COACHING

CONVERSATIONS

Read Up Jot Down™
Journaling Series

Ready yourself to learn

Eager to absorb new information

Accept new challenges

Digest and practice

Unleash your Powerful abilities

Jump at an opportunity to be
insightful

Open yourself to the experience

Transcribe your thoughts to words

*Deep understanding Of Who you are
in the Now*

Journaling

Coaching Conversations

How Anyone Can Use Proven Techniques To Breakthrough Barriers and Conquer Goals

Copyright ©2016 by Tina Frizzell-Jenkins
and Just Traders International, LLC (Updated December 2020)

ISBN: 978-0-9837312-6-9

Published by: JTI
JTI
P.O. Box 224
Glendale, MD.
20720CoachTinaFJ@jtillc.com

Editor: Dr. Joseph Amanfu
Cover Design and Illustration: Nada Orlic
Interior Design and Production: Alan Prescott

Printed in the USA

Disclaimer: This book is intended to enlighten the reader about the possibilities of coaching and to give the reader space to jot down his or her thoughts.

**Dedicated to the
Three "Ts"**

**Tinille, Tenise, & Trent
and
My Nieces and My Nephews**

Acknowledgments

I acknowledge my family and extended family for all their support in the creation of the first book in this journal series. I thank the creator of my creativity. I thank the Author Creator Cohort One for inspiring me. Thanks to Alan Prescott for his expertise in internal book design and Joseph Amanfu for editing mastery.

Table of Contents

READ UP

Chapter 1

What Is Coaching?

Coaching Is

Coaching is a distinctive dialogue that transforms your thinking and alters your actions. Coaching is an exciting profession that is regulated by the International Coach Federation (ICF). ICF defines coaching as, "partnering with clients in a thought-provoking and creative process that inspires them to maximize their personal and professional potential." Coaching is a creative experience, a method of personal discovery, and a journey taken with a professional friend. The experience blossoms as the client allows himself or herself to actively immerse in the activity of coaching. *Webster* defines experience as, "the skill or knowledge that you get by doing something." The coach facilitates the skill and knowledge-building by asking the discovery questions and by championing the client. These two ingredients, when added to the "doing something" or conscious action of the client, produces the learning shifts as the coach and the client take the journey together.

Coaching is a service that is offered for a number of different niches. A niche can be described as a specialty or area of expertise. The major specialties include but are not limited to, Life, Executive and Business coaching. Life coaching is broken down into a number of subcategories such as Life Purpose, Finance, Exercise, Relationship, Spiritual and Health and Wellness to name a few. Life coaching is typically centered on life issues and how the client adapts under the pressure as well as joys of life. Executive coaching encompasses leadership coaching, organizational coaching, work-life balance coaching, career coaching and change-management coaching. Business coaching includes start-up processes, foundation fundamentals, marketing strategies, customer focuses, strategic growth, balance lifestyle, and networking.

It is important to note that although there are several niches and sub-categories under the major areas of Life, Executive, and Business coaching as mentioned above, a Certified Professional Coach is considered an expert Generalist in the Coaching process. You may ask, "What does this mean?" It means that if you hire an Executive Coach and a relationship issue or growth opportunity arises, you can continue working with your Executive Coach, as the Certified Professional Coach is an expert in the coaching process. More information regarding ICF credentialing will be discussed in detail later.

Coaching History

It is often said that in order to know where you are going you need to know where you came from. Thus, a brief discussion of the roots of coaching is appropriate for a thorough understanding of the subject. I often hear statements like, "It seems like Leadership/Executive coaching popped up out of nowhere" or, "Sports coaching I know; I know nothing about this coaching." This is where the education begins—or does it? I believe I can safely say that at this point that most coaches attempt to define coaching. Then, when the eyebrows in front of us form that "V" shape and the eyes start to squint and we can sense their brain searching for a deeper understanding, we start to explain that coaching is not like counseling, consulting or mentoring. Just to get it out of the way, essentially, counseling has to do with healing past and present hurts while working with a professional; consulting has to do with taking direction from a professional; mentoring has to do with following a leader (broader explanation in Chapter 2); while coaching is about making your own way using the great potential within you.

In searching the Internet, it is difficult still to build a timeline of the growth of history relative to coaching; however, one author, Vikki G. Brock, completed an exceptionally detailed dissertation titled, GROUNDED THEORY OF THE ROOTS AND EMERGENCE OF COACHING.

Vikki G. Brock
A Dissertation
Submitted in Partial Fulfillment
  of the Requirements for the Degree
Doctor of Philosophy in Coaching and
  Human Development
International University of Professional
  Studies
Maui, 2008

I have highlighted and interpreted a few details from her writing below that shed light on the history of coaching. (Interested in a deeper understanding of the history of coaching? Google her.) That said, Ms. Grant traced coaching resources, though few, back to the late 1930s. In fact, she did a coaching book count, and between the years of 1978 and 1999 she was able to locate approximately 24 books specific to the topic of Coaching. Contrast those numbers to the approximately 29

Coaching books between 1998 and 2000. Surprisingly, in two years, we saw more books surface than the previous 29 years. This could candidly support the theory that coaching popped up out of nowhere. But as we are required to dig deeper when we seek the truth, Ms. Brock shows us journal writings on the subject much earlier. Coaching appears to have gradually, over the years, emerged from behavioral studies to an integral philosophy of equipping leaders to perform at a higher level to raise the bar of unlocking a person's potential with self-discovery.

It appears that the self-help era of the '90s really contributed to the growth of coaching. The following quote in Vikki's work acknowledges this notion: "The helping skills profession contributes to... coaching in numerous ways, providing, among other things, communication models, models for active listening, questioning techniques, empathic responding, and reflection. Techniques for challenging and exploring issues, as well as helping individuals to gain insight, also have enriched the practice of coaching" (Skiffington & Zeus, 2003, p. 16).

With a growth spurt really taking form by 1995, it is understandable how coach

Thomas Leonard seized the opportunity to start a non-profit organization to support fellow coaches and further promote coaching. Three years later, the International Coach Federation (ICF) was founded to bring awareness and structure to what is now a growing industry.

Fast forward to today, ICF is the largest and most respected organization of its kind. They advocate keeping ethics and skill development at the forefront of coaching. Additionally, ICF hosts global conventions to continue to unite the coaching community and provide cutting-edge, continuous learning opportunities.

Coaching Regulated by ICF

In a manner of speaking, the International Coach Federation (ICF) is to coaching institutions as the higher education accreditation board is to a university. It has taken on the responsibility of monitoring Coaching Programs and offers its stamp of accreditation to programs that meet the core coaching competencies. The ICF's coach credentialing systems have a three-year renewal system in place for coaches who carry ICF accreditation along with their coach school accreditation. The three types of accreditations available through ICF are Associate Certified Coach (ACC), Professional Certified Coach (PCC) and Master Certified Coach (MCC). Before obtaining a coaching certification at any level, coaches are required to pass a Coach Knowledge assessment. This exam determines that the coach has gained the skills and knowledge important to practice coaching and that the coach can demonstrate that he or she clearly understands the coaching core competencies and the Coaching Code of Ethics. ICF started in 1995 by Coach Thomas Leonard as a nonprofit organization. By 1998, the organization began its pursuit to change the outlook and the future of coaching. Indeed, coaching is on the rise with coaching being utilized in Fortune 500 companies, the Government, and individual engagements. Currently, ICF's credential membership is in excess of twenty thousand coaches and they are global. Lastly, ICF is a leading professional voice of the coaching community.

Visit www.coachfederation.org for the full story.

Coach-Client Chemistry & Venue

Coaching is best when the coach-client relationship has chemistry. Choosing a coach with chemistry is essential to a productive and lasting coaching relationship. This chemistry is similar to the draw you feel when meeting someone new and you can't quite explain it, but you know that the individual is meant to be in your life for a season or forever. You are willing to extend them a little more grace to peek into your personal space while hoping they will earn the right for you to allow them to speak into your life.

Coaching is practiced in person, via phone or virtually using tools like Skype. Individual coaching is one-on-one coaching. The client comes with the agenda and the coach takes a nonjudgmental approach to facilitating the powerful dialogue.

Group Coaching and Venue

Group coaching is a technique used with a small number of individuals striving to achieve a common goal. For example, it is a great follow-on activity to further learning initiatives or to support cultural change. This process is facilitated by a

Coach and generally there are 15 individuals or fewer in the group. The Coach is responsible for assisting the group in setting the rules and for holding the group accountable for maintaining the group rules of engagement, managing the discussion, keeping the energy up, asking powerful questions to aid the dialogue, and summarizing the action steps. The group members provide personal experiences, stories, support to other members, laughter, and best practices. Many prefer group coaching because there are several people in the "hot seat," so to speak, as opposed to one person during a one-on-one coaching session. Learning from this environment is not just on an individual one-on-one basis but is achieved through active listening of the other participants in the group.

The benefits of group coaching are as follows:
- Cost Savings
- Peer Learning
- Networking
- Group Support
- Less Individual Attention
- Social Learning
- Reflective Thought Time as Others Respond

Group Coaching occurs in person or virtually using tools like Skype, Adobe Connect or tele-conferencing. Again, the main ideas of Group Coaching are to deepening the learning or achieve a common goal relative to a specific topic in a group environment.

Seven Things to Consider Before Signing Coach-Client Agreement

The following are seven things to consider and discuss with the coach before signing a coaching agreement/hiring a coach:
1. Chemistry and trustworthiness
2. Coach's credentials and training
3. Coach's knowledge/experience in the niche you are seeking to develop
4. Coaching tools available to the coach
5. Coach's professional affiliations and networks
6. Coach's availability within your schedule
7. Your budget

5P Coaching: Purpose, Passion, Person, Personal Development & Product

Coaching is a methodology for discovering and tackling the "Five Ps": person, purpose, passion, personal development, and product creation and marketing.

Understanding oneself as a unique person and walking out one's purpose is foundational for most individuals who want to actively contribute to mankind and society. Using coaching, the client, in partnership with a coach, has the ability to unfold complex layers of the client's life that cause the client to interpret their reason(s) for being. Passion can almost always be tied back to one's purpose. Passion, on the other hand, is generally easier to reveal and build upon. Maximizing one's potential in one's passion is definitely a coachable topic.

Personal development brings an enormous silo of topics to add value to the client. Personal development stretches and strengthens the client at a pace and intellectual level that suits the client.

Lastly, product development is shaping a physical invention or intellectual property from conception to market by alleviating fears, maximizing potential, increasing confidence or making appreciable improvements on what already exists.

Coaching the 5 Ps can offer a fresh perspective that elicits a client to produce solutions and strategies while working towards a predetermined goal.

Coaching Acrostic Summary

Coaching is, by design, a unique relationship that is empowered by a powerful process of dialogue.

C — Confidentiality and Chemistry

O — Oops - missed opportunity if offered coaching and you decline

A — Aha moments that coaching brings like the room going from dark to light in a moment

C — Consulting or giving advice and Counseling or healing are NOT Coaching

H — How do I empower myself to develop and transform?

I — I resist the ordinary by pressing forward with a plan to accomplish my goals and dreams

N — Not mentoring

G — Getting excited about your personal development; if you don't get excited about it, no one else will!

Coaching & Seminars

Bonus Question Activity

1. What is coaching?

2. What type of a coach will best serve you?

3. When will you start on your coaching journey?

3. Meditate/reflect/answer

2. Meditate/reflect/answer

1. Coaching is a distinctive dialogue that transforms your thinking and alters your actions.

Chapter 2

Coaching versus Mentoring

Coaching is NOT Mentoring

Coaching is about making your way and putting your stamp/hand-print on the event, goal or thing, while mentoring is about following someone else's way, staying on the path they have charted, skipping the minefields they encountered, and getting their results or something similar. Coaching, by design, creates the space to launch your innovations and creativity while mapping your own path. Coaching believes that what you have within you is all that you need to be the best you possible.

Checking the definition of a mentor, *Webster* says, "someone who teaches or gives help and advice to a less experienced and often younger person."

Mentoring Demo

The following is an example of a dialogue between a mentor and a mentee:

Mentee: Kevin, good to see you today.

Mentor: Good of you to drop by, Andrea.

Mentee: How did you decide to be an electrical engineer? What path led you to your college and to be a successful engineer at NASA?

Mentor: Wow that's a mouthful.

Mentee: I am truly interested in becoming an electrical, mechanical or civil engineer and working for NASA.

Mentor: That is an excellent goal, if I say so myself. I started much like you, being diligent with my studies in high school and taking the college preparatory classes.

Mentee: Yes, I have Calculus, Advanced Chemistry and Physics this year.

Mentor: A good path to take, as I did towards electrical engineering

Mentee: How do I know which discipline to pursue?

Mentor: I was a little torn between electrical and mechanical, so I did a little research and the electrical jobs at the time were a little more in demand and they were paying better; so I went with electrical engineering.

Mentee: What college did you choose and why?

Mentor: I chose Northeastern University (NU) in Boston, Massachusetts because of their Cooperative (Co-op) Education program that my mentor turned me on to applying for.

Mentee: What is a co-op program?

Mentor: A co-op program is a program where you mix your education with hands-on experience by alternating learning with work in your field. The program took five years, but I graduated with a degree and experience, which gave me an edge entering into the marketplace after graduation.

Mentee: What company did you work with in your co-op program?

Mentor: I worked with a military electronic company located in Falls Church, Virginia, called E-Systems, Melpar Division.

Mentee: After graduation, did you go to work for NASA?

Mentor: No, I went to work for Melpar where I developed my electrical skills and my leadership skills.

Mentee: Did you go to NASA next?

Mentor: No, there was a freeze on government hires at NASA, so I went to a couple of other companies, sharpening my skills and building my confidence. Then I landed a position with McDonald Douglas on a NASA contract. After much success at McDonald Douglas, I interviewed with NASA and accepted a job as an electrical engineer. I did not come into NASA straight out of college, but I believe my stint working for a NASA contractor allowed me to showcase my abilities and secure an interview with the company of my dreams.

Mentee: That's good information. Now I know another path in case I do not get in straight out of college.

Mentor: True.

Mentee: What should I avoid or stay away from as I pursue working for NASA if I don't get in straight out of college?

Mentor: Try to avoid companies that do not have contracts with NASA. Though you might gain good skills with those other companies, the companies with the NASA contracts offer the best opportunities to get into NASA.

Mentee: What other advice do you have to offer?

Mentor: Get connected with good study teams in college and have some fun there, but keep the fun limited since you will have plenty of time to have fun once you reach your goal and become an engineer.

Mentee: That sounds fair. I will study hard and keep partying at an all-time low for me.

Mentor: Good, you will do great. Call me anytime. I am going to connect you to a couple of my contacts if you decide to go to NU and if you decide to go anywhere else, I may have a contact there, too.

Mentee: I can't thank you enough.

Mentor: It is my pleasure.

Mentee: I will be in touch.

Mentor: So long for now.

Mentee: So long.

Coaching Demo

Using the same basic scenario, let's follow a coaching dialogue.

As a reminder, we defined coaching as a distinctive dialogue that transforms your thinking and alters your actions.

Coach: Good day, Andrea.

Client: How is it going, Coach Kevin?

Coach: Wonderful, and how are you?

Client: No complaints.

Coach: What is on your agenda for today's session?

Client: It's decision time. I need to chart a

career path and identify a college to attend. I am interested in engineering but I am not sure what area of engineering to pursue.

Coach: To be sure I understand you correctly: you need to choose a major in college and a college to attend. You have an interest in engineering but you are not sure what discipline.

Client: That's it.

Coach: Over these next few sessions, if we can chart a journey for your college career, how much value would you place on our time together?

Client: A lot of value.

Coach: What opinion would you have about the fee your parents are paying me?

Client: It would be worth every dollar.

Coach: Engineering is pretty intense. What end goal do you have in mind?

Client: Ultimately, I want to be a NASA engineer.

Coach: That sounds exciting. How long has this been a dream of yours?

Client: It has been a dream of mine since I was about ten when I saw a documentary of the first man landing on the moon.

Coach: Tell me more about what you saw in the documentary that made you think NASA engineering can be a part of your future?

Client: They talked about the cool robotics of the future and how engineers would play a major part in creating the robots that would help advance science.

Coach: What do you know about robotics and the types of engineers that are likely to work on it?

Client: I believe electrical engineers will have a lot to do with the movement of the robots because they have to be wired up with different circuits and stuff. I think the mechanical engineer may actually design the physical components of the robot.

Coach: That sounds close to accurate. I noticed that you had an energy spike when you spoke about designing the robot. What about designing the actual robot gets you excited?

Client: I think it would be super cool to figure out if the robot has a face and to determine how many fingers it needs to affectively pick up stuff in space.

Coach: What classes have you taken up to this point to prepare you to embark on an engineering program?

Client: I have taken the entire college preparatory course curriculum with an emphasis on math and science.

Coach: Great job on your thinking ahead and taking action to assist your dreams in coming true!

Client: Thanks!

Coach: When we started talking you mentioned that you were not sure which discipline in engineering you wanted to pursue. However, you were pretty excited about mechanical engineering. What makes you unsure of mechanical engineering?

Client: My professor says it is hard to get employment at NASA and to have a backup plan and I read that electrical engineers earn a better living.

Coach: What was the salary differential between electrical and mechanical engineering from your research?

Client: In some cases, it was as little as a couple of thousand dollars to as much as ten thousand dollars.

Coach: On a scale of 1 to 10, with 10 being the most desirable, how important is it at this point in your life that you have a career that excites you?

Client: 10!

Coach: Keeping a 10 in mind, how much would it be worth making a few thousand dollars less and being excited about your career?

Client: It would be worth making less to be happier.

Coach: What discipline of engineering would you like to pursue in college?

Client: Mechanical engineering with an emphasis on robotics.

Coach: Yeah! You did it. You discovered the best engineering path for you at this point.

Client: I guess I did.

Coach: We have a little time left. Let's start our discussion about your university of choice. Eventually, we will discuss your choice of employer. How does this sound for our path moving forward?

Client: That sounds great.

Coach: When you think university, what comes up for you?

Client: Lots of things. Tuition cost, not too many students, roommates, out of state, doing something new, weekend visits home, etc.

Coach: I heard you say not too many

students. How would you classify size-wise "not too many students"?

Client: A small to medium university so I have a better chance at getting to know the professors and students.

Coach: What types of programs appeal to you that the university should offer like early entrance, co-op, housing for scholars, etc.

Client: I have no idea. I have not thought of that.

Coach: For homework, do some Google searches and write down 3 to 5 items that appeal to you that you would like at the university of your choice.

Client: I can do that.

Coach: How would you describe our time together today?

Client: Deep and yet inspiring.

Coach: You inspire me, being so young and on top of your life game plan. See you in three weeks.

Client: Yes, thanks and see ya!

Coach or Mentor, Your Agenda Please

Let's examine the two different scenarios played out above. The mentor is clearly laying out a path that the student can take that is much like his own. He shares some benefits, things to avoid and some life lessons. Clearly, he is interested in her success to be much like his. The mentor offers to make connections for her to ease her way.

Contrast: the coach is inquisitive. The questions he asked are less about clarifying information for himself and more about the client's filtering and understanding her own thoughts and ideas. The client is doing the work. and the coach is providing the guidance necessary with powerful questions to assist the client in reaching her goal, with the intent of her actions to be sustainable.

How exciting to watch her have aha moments and make mental shifts due to her potential being unfurled by self-discoveries.

Bonus Question Activity

1. How do a coach and mentor differ?

2. How are a coach and mentor alike?

3. Who establishes the agenda for the coaching session?

3. The Client.

service.

providing a developmental

2. They both commit to

making the way.

way; a coach assists you in

1. A mentor shows you the

Chapter 3

Coaching Techniques, Tools, Goal Conquering, and Self-Coaching Questions

Coaching Techniques

Coaches can use a number of different techniques throughout the developmental and discovery journey with a client. We will review a few, like types of questioning, The 3-Step Coaching Process and Laser Coaching.

The use of open-ended questions as opposed to closed-ended questions is a primary technique. Closed-ended questions drive yes or no answers. Yes or no answers are not desirable, as they limit the depth of thought and restrict the conversation. On the other hand, open-ended questions solicit thought, deep thinking, and pondering. This is the type of behavior that the coach is delighted to receive. The client is more engaged in the conversation; thus, has a better opportunity to have the "aha" moments, make shifts or completely buy into new or different behaviors that are lasting and sustainable.

The 3-Step Coaching Process (from my iPEC education) is a technique that explores (1) what is working well; (2) why it is working well and (3) what specifically made it work. The technique helps you to build on your previously discovered strengths, resources, and gifts to achieve a current goal. The way this technique works is: as an issue or obstacle arises in life that seems unmovable or unbeatable, you reflect back to a point in time where you overcame an obstacle and you remember what it was like to get the victory. You remember what you saw, what you smelled, what you heard, what you felt and perhaps you remember how good the victory meal was you enjoyed after the ordeal. You use those feelings of success to create the energy physically and mentally to walk through the current trial/test to the other side.

Breakthrough Laser Coaching (from my iPEC education) is another technique. It is not so much about speed but focus, inner-block removal and creating new possibilities. This technique skillfully guides clients using thoughts, feelings and actions, helping a client validate a current situation, behavior or desire. Then the client is assisted in shifting the situation, behavior, or desire to a new desirable belief and then to sustain the action with accountability.

Coaching Tools

Coaches use tools and assessments to assist the client in reaching his or her goals. For instance, the Wheel of Life is a good tool to use when the client's working through narrowing down real-life issues that could use the most attention and development at that moment of time in their life. The wheel essentially gives the client a visual of the major aspects of life. The client rates each aspect, and those parts of life that they score low are possible areas for developing. They can choose to develop using coaching.

Wheel of Life

JTI Wheel of Life for Worklife Balance

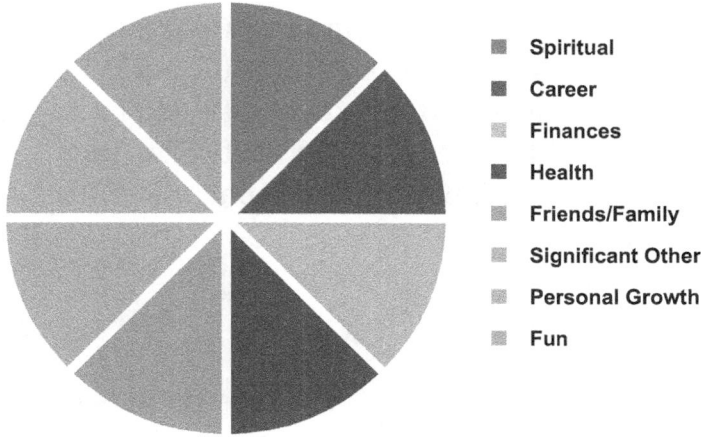

- Spiritual
- Career
- Finances
- Health
- Friends/Family
- Significant Other
- Personal Growth
- Fun

JTI Wheel of Life
for Worklife Balance—
Client Adjusted

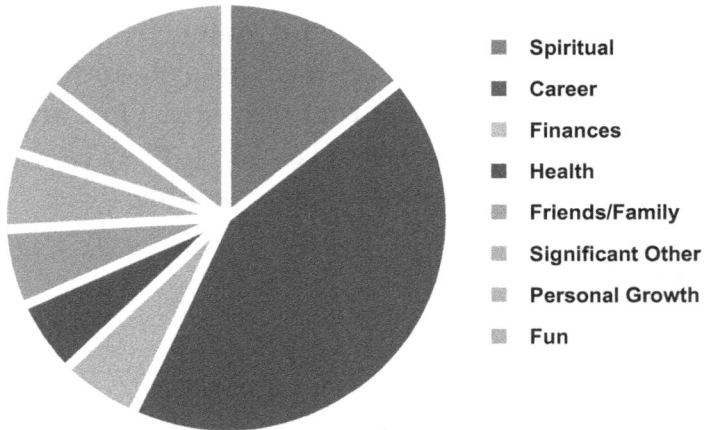

- Spiritual
- Career
- Finances
- Health
- Friends/Family
- Significant Other
- Personal Growth
- Fun

The adjusted wheel depicts a client's life balance. The client has self-rated his lifestyle. Giving each category from 1 to 10 points depending on how much of his time is spent in that particular area. As you can see, this individual's career is out of balance with the rest of his life. This could be cause for coaching if the client elects.

Wheel of Business

Much like the Wheel of Life, the Wheel of Business empowers business owners to access the working components of the business and determine what areas of their business might need "stepping up" to improve the bottom line/profit.

JTI Wheel of Business

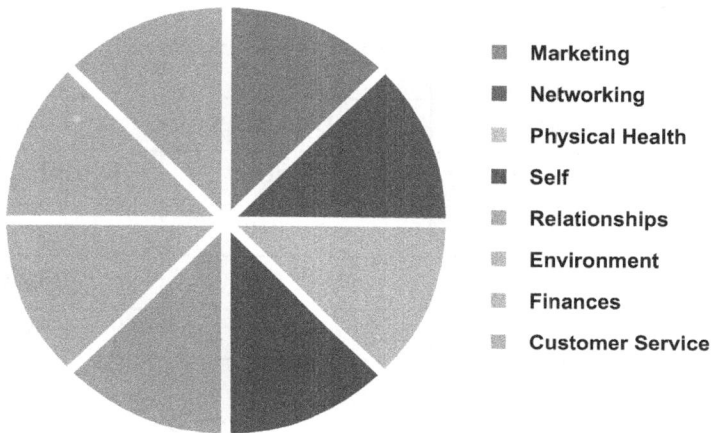

- ▨ Marketing
- ▨ Networking
- ▨ Physical Health
- ▨ Self
- ▨ Relationships
- ▨ Environment
- ▨ Finances
- ▨ Customer Service

Each category can be self-rated on a sliding scale from 1 to 10 with 10 denoting that this aspect of the business is on point. Any category rated under a 7 could be cause for coaching if the client elects.

Values Tool

Another tool a coach uses is a Value Assessment Tool. This is generally a written exercise that is completed, scored and debriefed. Our values dictate a lot, if not most, of our actions. Therefore, spending some time self-evaluating values is a good exercise for everyone. Below is a list of values to contemplate and meditate on for self-clarity (no self-judging required).

VALUES LIST

Manners	Love	Practicality
Family	Community	Security
Spirituality	Justice	Reliability
Honesty	Loyalty	Fitness
Service	Generosity	Legacy
Equality	Inner Harmony	Compassion

Complete the sentence below by filling in a value from above. You can also choose some values not listed and see what comes up for you.

I value _____

Because _____

_____

_____

49 Self-Coaching Questions

Self-coaching questions are good questions to ask yourself when you are working towards accomplishing a goal, contemplating what's next for you and the family, or in preparation for having a conversation with a coach, to name a few. Below are 49 questions to use in self-coaching situations:

Personal Growth

1. On a scale of 1 to 10 with ten being the greatest, how important is it to navigate your personal development?

2. How much time per week are you willing to dedicate to developing yourself?

3. What subject of personal development do you wish to pursue?

4. How much of your budget are you willing to allocate for your educational pursuits?

5. What type of coach will you seek?

6. Who is your mentor and who are you mentoring?

7. What is driving your pursuit of your advanced education?

Career

1. How satisfied are you in your current career?

2. What is your ideal career?

3. What financial sacrifices are you willing to take to work a job you love that does not pay the salary you desire?

4. What could you do along with your job to give your life more meaning?

5. What business have you considered to advance your financial goals?

6. How many years do you plan to work for someone else?

7. What are the fears that keep you from launching your business?

Relationships

1. What would you say is your best relationship?

2. How well do you get along with your co-workers?

3. How much do you value family?

4. How much time is dedicated to enhancing your life with your significant other?

5. What kind of friend would your friends say you are?

6. What kind of friend are you striving to be?

7. What are your top 3 relationship values?

Entertainment

1. What do you like to do for fun?

2. What have you not made time to do that you feel would be entertaining?

3. How much time in your schedule is

dedicated to doing the things you enjoy?

4. How often do you get together with your hobby community?

5. What type of vacation do you consider enjoyable?

6. How often do you take vacation?

7. Where would you like to go that you have never been?

Physical Health

1. How many days a week do you exercise?

2. What exercise feels the least like work?

3. When was your last yearly physical exam?

4. What will it take for you to dedicate 4 to 5 nights a week to purposely eat healthy?

5. What is the process you have in place with your exercise accountability partner to help you stay on track?

6. What is your system for drinking 6 to 8 glasses of water a day?

7. What 2 junk foods can you eliminate from your diet while you meet your weight-loss goal?

Finances

1. How often do you work with a budget that has been developed especially for your life?

2. How much of your income have you dedicated to your faith and to charity?

3. What is a long-term savings goal and how much of your income is dedicated to that goal?

4. What is a short-term savings goal?

5. What activity could you put on hold to dedicate those funds to reaching your financial goal?

6. How have you expanded your savings portfolio outside of the normal banking institutions?

7. What actions are you willing to put in place to have a financial mentor by the end of the month?

Spiritual

1. Who is your spiritual accountability partner?

2. How much time daily do you dedicate to being quiet and listening?

3. What practice do you have in place to advance your spirituality?

4. How often do you assemble with other believers to worship?

5. What behaviors are fundamental to elevate your faith?

6. What thoughts have you given to formal spiritual training?

7. What has your spiritual mentor given you guidance to do but you have put off for a later time?

Bonus Question Activity

1. What is an open-ended question?

2. What is a closed-ended question?

3. What is a coaching tool a client can request from their coach to evaluate their life?

3. Wheel of Life

2. A question that yields a
yes or no answer

1. A question that yields a
conversation

Chapter 4

Coach Tina FJ:
Life Journey to Coaching

Life Journey to Coaching

According to a bestselling book, "**God is able to make all grace abound to you, so that in all things at all times; having all that you need, you may abound in every good work.**"

Webster defines the word *abound* as to be plentiful, to exist in large numbers, to be filled, having abundance and being wealthy. Therefore, if we insert the definition into the scripture it would read something like this: "God is able to make grace plentiful to you, so that in all things at all times; having all that you need, you may be plentiful or wealthy in every good work." Wow! I believe every life has a purpose. Couple life's purpose with grace and awesome things are possible...and they occur; my life/my journey speaks to that.

I am a Washingtonian. I was born and raised in our great nation's capital Washington, DC. My loving and highly supportive parents are Tillman and Aretha Frizzell. Mom still lives in the house they built for us in the city. Dad went home to be with the Lord in January 2012. I was born the middle child between two delightful brothers that I affectionately call Tony and Lil' Till (5'11-1/2") and who contributed to making life growing up interesting and fun. My maternal grandparents lived in the house next door and I had a host of other relatives living nearby. On many memorable occasions, several of those relatives, if not all, would convene on the porch and in the yard of my grand-parents. A lot of laughter and family discussions took place there. I like to believe that my grandfather's quiet, loving and gentle nature contributed to my demeanor while my grandmother's creativity and faith registered on my radar at an early age.

I was educated in the public school system where the great majority of my teachers were nurturing, caring and all-around great educators. In elementary school, it became obvious that learning would be a challenge to me. It was in third grade where two teachers pulled me aside and quizzed me on some basic math. They asked, "What is seven plus seven?" I would reply quickly 14. Then they would ask, "What is seven plus eight?" I would hesitate, think and calculate to get the answer of 15. They would quiz me on several like problems where they would get the same responses. It was clear to them that I should have been able to respond just as quick to the second question as I did the

first because I had only to realize that I
needed to add one to my previous answer
to get the next answer. I remember seeing
the puzzlement in their eyes and hearing
the comment of, "She does not get it."
They didn't get that I learned differently.
Different is not bad; it is just different. I
have Dyslexia *(rear-view reflection,
coaching moment)*.

It was also around that same time that I
remember working with a speech
therapist to assist me in speaking
correctly. Add to that the fact that
reading and reading comprehension were
thorns in my educational existence. In
sixth grade, I was chosen to give the
sixth-grade graduation Welcome Address
where I received a standing ovation. I also
remember getting several acknowledg-
ments and awards. This was another
moment in time when the greatness
within me superseded what appeared
*(rear-view reflection, coaching
moment)*.

That journey of my life was the
first in confirming that *God is able to
make all grace abound to me, so that in
all things at all times; having all that I
need, I may be plentiful.* Grace put the
correct people in my life to assist me in
my learning challenges. Grace gave me
parents who inspired me. Grace brought
out my ability to remember things

whether I understood them or not. Grace provided me with the platform to give a speech and build my confidence.

It was in junior high school where I met my high school sweetheart, the wonderful man I have been married to for the past 30-plus years after dating all through high school and college. I worked hard in junior high to keep a B/B+ average and that is also where my athletic abilities flourished. Track and field and basketball were my sports of choice. I excelled in track because I was quick and though I was not much of a shooter in basketball, I was a great defensive player and could steal the ball. I was good at sports but I did not love them. Perhaps I had the ability but I did not have the passion to be great.

Sports introduced me to athletic coaching. I adored my coaches and the way they motivated me to be my best. I could understand how being a part-time coach like my dad could be an appealing thing to do someday, but being the athlete I could take it or leave it... mostly leave it. Motivating others was appealing *(rear view reflection, coaching moment)*. Oddly enough, I was more interested in getting academic awards than trophies and medals.

By the time I graduated from junior high, I was sure I wanted to conquer the academic monster of learning. It was Grace that gave me direction in this season of my life. It was Grace that afforded me the gall to presume that I could accentuate that part of me, my intellect, which appeared not to be my best.

It was in high school, H.D. Woodson, that I had the time of my life. I was voted the friendliest in our senior yearbook. I developed friendships that I still cherish today. I was inducted into the National Honor Society in my junior year. I graduated number 19 in my class of over six hundred and I was vice president of my graduating class. Don't get me wrong; I believe I had to study twice as hard as everyone else to get the results I achieved.

It was in high school that I decided to pursue engineering in college after completing a summer program in engineering at Howard University and working on and solving an engineering traffic project in the city through a program at the school. However, I had a high school math teacher who told me I was not engineering material. Although I was doing well in math, it was too much of a struggle for me and I would not make it through engineering math. The comment stung but I was familiar with the concept called Grace.

I went on to college where the road was rough and the obstacles were plentiful. Fun was in limited quantities and it was there that I had an advisor who suggested I take another career path. My struggles were not worth it in his opinion. During this journey of my life, my mom would regularly send me positive affirmations to display around my room from Success Motivation Institute, a franchise she acquired. Therefore, I reached back into my memory and recalled that *God is able to make all grace abound to me, so that in all things at all times; having all that I need, I may abound in every good work.*

I finished my undergraduate work in December 1983 and walked with the Class of 1984 with a BS in Mechanical Engineering from Northeastern University. At that time, it was the largest private institution with the best cooperative education program. Upon graduation, I had a year-and-a-half of on-the-job experience that afforded me the opportunity to obtain a job with a very nice entry-level salary for that time. As an aside, I recall going to the bank to cash my check and getting speculative glances when the bank teller would glance at the amount, then at my identification and back at me. I was a twenty-three-year-old (I looked more like eighteen) African American female with a substantial paycheck for that time. You might imagine that bankers were a little skeptical.

I started my professional career in the private sector in January 1984. I worked for a company called E-System, Melpar Division in Falls Church, VA. This was the same company I worked for as a co-op student, starting in 1981. The company's production was military electronics. The following September, I was married to Willis at our family church, Ward Memorial AME in the District of Columbia. My husband and I both enjoyed employment at E-Systems until May of 1989 when I started government employment with NASA, Goddard Space Flight Center in Greenbelt, Maryland as a Facilities Engineer. This position's responsibility was to create and maintain the state-of-the-art laboratories and buildings such that the best science and missions happened as scheduled.

In November of 1989, our first daughter, Tinille, was born and in 1993 we welcomed our second daughter, Tenise.

In 1994, my husband joined me as a Government employee at NASA working on the mission as an electrical engineer.

In 1995, I requested and received a General Contractor's permit to build our second home that my husband and I designed. Imagine with me the excitement of being able to build my own home. This is something I had dreamed of as a young child. I went through the county's permitting process and was approved. Our finances were in order. I put together, and I quote, "one of the best loan packages I have ever seen." This is what the bank agent said. She told me everything looked great and she only had to go to the vice president to get a cursory signature. She said it would be no problem because everything was in order.

She called me back with hesitation and amazement in her voice. She said Mr. VP would not sign and there were no reasons given. I talked to the vice president, and to make a long story short, he did not believe in me despite my qualifications. He offered to loan me as much money as I needed to *purchase* a house. I was not interested in his offer. I felt I was being mistreated because I was a young Black female—and it hurt.

Around that time, Mom had to remind me of Grace and she advised me to contact my Congressman. The very next day after the vice president was contacted by the Congressman's office, my construction build loan was miraculously approved. The vice president called to let me know and to threaten me with, "I will not give you a cent more for overruns." Grace not only got us building but Grace allowed us to get our U & O (Use & Occupancy) in seven months with a few thousand left in the bank. In my life, this was one of the "all things" that Grace abounded in.

Prior to starting a new professional career path as a facilities engineer, I started a private career path as a home-business owner that would eventually lead me twenty-plus years later to the Institute for Professional Excellence in Coaching (iPEC). Along with my husband, I started a service company called Advance Auto Consultants, Inc. The company assisted mostly women in the purchase of a new car without the haggling and at a great price. The service was needed because it was a known fact, especially at the time: those women were being taken advantage of when purchasing a car.

It was at this point in my life/our lives that it became obvious that we had to earn how to keep the money we were making and not let taxes consume the fruits of our labor. We also discovered that it was necessary to attach ourselves to mentors who could teach us what most people never thought to know or knew to learn. Later, we would start another service company called Just Traders International (JTI), LLC. This became the umbrella company for transportation services and other home-based business services. Through these business experiences and attaching ourselves to the correct people, we were able to put some practices in place that became worth sharing so others could benefit.

I started giving a financial PowerPoint presentation in my basement that not only encouraged families and home-based business owners to keep the money they earned but it taught them how. We worked on budgets, documenting business expenditures and igniting passions through business ventures. As you may imagine, the seminars grew to the point that they were being hosted in libraries, meeting rooms and hotels.

Not only did the seminars grow, but also people started requesting individual support. While providing support, it became clear that I could better serve my clients if I could offer an additional skillset that I recognized to be coaching.

It wasn't enough at this point to provide awareness, give direction, and mentor. I became interested in having my clients buy into their own success and the process to get there. Working with a coach could do that for the client. My first introduction to a coach was in a NASA-sponsored leadership program called Accelerated Leadership Development. The twenty of us accepted into the program were given personal coaches for two years. Those sessions with my coach caused the "aha" moments that led me to want to be a certified coach.

As life would have it, I was becoming more and more dissatisfied with my NASA engineering/planning job. I no longer felt I was making a significant contribution and a call came out to become a NASA coach. As I read the bulletin, it was as if the Coach's Council was asking for me personally. It was a way to enhance my career at NASA while incorporating my outside life interest that I really enjoyed.

However, I interviewed and the panel rejected me. In summation, I was told that I lacked similar background knowledge and I did not have the on-the-job experience of developing an individual like a supervisor role would afford someone. I was crushed to tears. The panel did not see in me what I saw in myself. I felt like I had failed myself, and all of the people I was supposed to walk along side of and assist them to reach their potential. Somehow, I had fallen off course and surely jeopardized fulfilling my purpose. Then I remembered, *God is able to make all grace abound to me, so that in all things at all times; having all that I need, I may abound in every good work.*

Good work in this case was coaching and I believed that I could be and would be plentiful; I pursued coaching as a self-improvement with the support of my management. I found coaching to be the most awesome and rewarding self-development I had ever done and I have enjoyed numerous self-growth classes over the years.

Approximately a little more than half-way through the program it became absolutely evident to me that I would be a coach. My pursuit of coaching and willingness to fulfill the quest on my own got the attention of NASA's Coaching Council. Once I became certified, I was invited to be a member with them. I accepted the invitation and I was pleased to collaborate with the bench in 2008.

After moving from performing engineering tasks to working with engineering training programs, I migrated to Human Resources. Today, I am the Coaching Program Manager for NASA Goddard Space Flight Center. We have an active bench with internal and external coaches. We are honored that several private-sector and government entities seek to model our program. *God is able to make all grace abound to you, so that in all things at all times; having all that you need, you may abound in every good work.*

Within the coaching community, coaching is done using different styles, skills, and techniques. Planting seeds (inch by inch life is a cinch), visioning, and celebrating are a few skills my mom successfully put into practice with me growing up. Also, I am particularly drawn to a coaching technique called The 3-Step Coaching Process (refer to the process in Chapter 3). This is a technique that I have been practicing from a very young age not knowing it to be used in the coaching world.

Reiterating the way this technique works, as an issue or obstacle arises in life that seems unmovable or unbeatable, you reflect back to a point in time when you overcame an obstacle and you remember what it was like to get the victory. You remember what you saw, what you smelled, what you heard, what you felt and perhaps you remember how good the victory meal was you enjoyed after the ordeal. You use those feelings of success to create the energy physically and mentally to walk through the current trail to the other side. The other side is success. For me, that's when I relied on past triumphs that the victories stemmed from Grace. Why? Because, *God is able to make all grace abound to you, so that in all things at all times; having all that you need, you may abound in every good work.*

Coaching is a good work. Coaching is a service, and serving feeds my soul. Coaching is a piece of the puzzle of my life that makes me who I am. Therefore, **I applaud IPEC in creating a spectacular program that uniquely prepared me to be a professional friend**. I am someone who provides ongoing client stimulation and, encouragement for personal improvement while facilitating guidance towards life's purposes and goals. I am an empowerment coach who specializes in executive, leadership, home-based business and coaching.
Visit www.jticoaching.com to learn more.

Bonus Question Activity

1. What coaching technique did Coach Tina FJ use throughout her life?

2. What coaching school did Coach Tina FJ attend?

3. What is Coach Tina FJ's website address?

3. jfjcoaching.com

2. iPEC

1. 3-Step Coaching Process

JOT DOWN

Journaling Begins

Session Date: _____

Coach: _____**Time:** _____

Agenda: _____

_____

_____

_____

_____

Aha Moment: _____

_____

_____

_____

Assignments:_____

_____

_____

_____

_____

_____

_____

_____

"Passion is an energy injection." ~Tina Frizzell-Jenkins

Reflections: _____

_____

_____

_____

_____

_____

_____

_____

_____

_____

_____

_____

_____

_____

_____

_____

_____

_____

_____

_____

*"When you have confidence, you have a lot of fun. And
when you have fun, you can do amazing things."*
~Joe Namath

Session Date: _____

Coach: _____ **Time:** _____

Agenda: _____

_____

_____

_____

_____

Aha Moment: _____

_____

_____

_____

Assignments: _____

_____

_____

_____

_____

_____

_____

_____

"What holds most people back isn't the quality of their ideas, but their lack of faith in themselves. You have to live your life as if you are already where you want to be."
~Russell Simmons

Reflections: _____

_____

_____

_____

_____

_____

_____

_____

_____

_____

_____

_____

_____

_____

_____

_____

_____

_____

_____

_____

"As the physically weak man can make himself strong by careful and patient training, so the man of weak thoughts can make them strong by exercising himself in right thinking." ~James Allen

Session Date: _____

Coach: _____**Time:** _____

Agenda: _____

_____

_____

_____

_____

Aha Moment: _____

_____

_____

_____

Assignments:_____

_____

_____

_____

_____

_____

_____

_____

"If I could be in the moment over the horizon, then in that same moment, I would be in awe." ~**Tina Frizzell-Jenkins**

Reflections: _____

_____

_____

_____

_____

_____

_____

_____

_____

_____

_____

_____

_____

_____

_____

_____

_____

_____

"Of course motivation is not permanent. But then, neither is bathing; but it is something you should do on a regular basis." ~Zig Ziglar

Session Date: _____

Coach: _____**Time:** _____

Agenda: _____

_____

_____

_____

_____

Aha Moment: _____

_____

_____

_____

Assignments: _____

_____

_____

_____

_____

_____

_____

_____

*"For lack of wood the fire goes out, and where there is no whisperer contention quiets down." ~**Proverb 26:20 NKJ***

Reflections: _____

_____

_____

_____

_____

_____

_____

_____

_____

_____

_____

_____

_____

_____

_____

_____

_____

_____

_____

_____

_____

"Discipline is the bridge between goals and accomplishment." ~Jim Rohn

Session Date: _____

Coach: _____**Time:** _____

Agenda: _____

_____

_____

_____

_____

Aha Moment: _____

_____

_____

_____

Assignments:_____

_____

_____

_____

_____

_____

_____

_____

"Out of the abundance of the heart the mouth speaketh."
~Matthew 12:34 NKJ

Reflections: _____

_____

_____

_____

_____

_____

_____

_____

_____

_____

_____

_____

_____

_____

_____

_____

_____

"You have within you right now, everything you need to deal with whatever the world can throw at you." ~Brian Tracy

Session Date: _____

Coach: _____ **Time:** _____

Agenda: _____

_____

_____

_____

_____

Aha Moment: _____

_____

_____

_____

Assignments: _____

_____

_____

_____

_____

_____

_____

_____

"Let every man be swift to hear, slow to speak."
~James 1:19 NKJ

Reflections: _____

_____

_____

_____

_____

_____

_____

_____

_____

_____

_____

_____

_____

_____

_____

_____

_____

_____

"The secret of getting ahead is getting started."
~Mark Twain

Session Date: _____

Coach: _____**Time:** _____

Agenda: _____

_____

_____

_____

_____

Aha Moment: _____

_____

_____

_____

Assignments:_____

_____

_____

_____

_____

_____

_____

"Tell the truth and shame the devil."
~Dr. Vivian M. Jackson

Reflections: _____

_____

_____

_____

_____

_____

_____

_____

_____

_____

_____

_____

_____

_____

_____

_____

_____

_____

_____

_____

"I can't change the direction of the wind, but I can adjust my sails to always reach my destination." ~Jimmy Dean

Session Date: _____

Coach: _____ **Time:** _____

Agenda: _____

_____

_____

_____

_____

Aha Moment: _____

_____

_____

_____

Assignments: _____

_____

_____

_____

_____

_____

_____

_____

_____

"Quiet people are often misunderstood but they are rarely stupid" ~Unknown

Reflections: _____

_____

_____

_____

_____

_____

_____

_____

_____

_____

_____

_____

_____

_____

_____

_____

_____

_____

_____

_____

_____

"Most people want to avoid pain, and discipline is usually painful." ~John C. Maxwell

Session Date: _____

Coach: _____ **Time:** _____

Agenda: _____

_____

_____

_____

_____

Aha Moment: _____

_____

_____

_____

Assignments: _____

_____

_____

_____

_____

_____

_____

_____

"Life is like riding a bicycle. To keep your balance, you must keep moving." ~**Albert Einstein**

Reflections: _____

_____

_____

_____

_____

_____

_____

_____

_____

_____

_____

_____

_____

_____

_____

_____

_____

_____

"You know you are on the road to success if you would do your job, and not be paid for it." **~Oprah Winfrey**

Session Date: _____

Coach: _____ **Time:** _____

Agenda: _____

_____

_____

_____

_____

Aha Moment: _____

_____

_____

_____

Assignments: _____

_____

_____

_____

_____

_____

_____

"The price of anything is the amount of life you exchange for it." ~Henry David Thoreau

Reflections: _____

_____
_____
_____
_____
_____
_____
_____
_____
_____
_____
_____
_____
_____
_____
_____
_____
_____
_____

"Faith is taking the first step even when you don't see the whole staircase." ~Martin Luther King, Jr.

Session Date: _____

Coach: _____**Time:** _____

Agenda: _____

_____

_____

_____

_____

Aha Moment: _____

_____

_____

_____

Assignments:_____

_____

_____

_____

_____

_____

_____

_____

"Life is too short for long-term grudges." ~**Elon Musk**

Reflections: _____

_____
_____
_____
_____
_____
_____
_____
_____
_____
_____
_____
_____
_____
_____
_____
_____
_____
_____
_____

"Try to be a rainbow in someone's cloud." ~Maya Angelou

Session Date: _____

Coach: _____ **Time:** _____

Agenda: _____

_____

_____

_____

_____

Aha Moment: _____

_____

_____

_____

Assignments: _____

_____

_____

_____

_____

_____

_____

_____

"He who has a why to live can bear almost any how."
~Friedrich Nietzsche

Reflections: _____

_____

_____

_____

_____

_____

_____

_____

_____

_____

_____

_____

_____

_____

_____

_____

_____

_____

_____

_____

_____

"In order to attain the impossible, one must attempt the absurd." ~Miguel de Cervantes

Session Date: _____

Coach: _____**Time:** _____

Agenda: _____

_____

_____

_____

_____

Aha Moment: _____

_____

_____

_____

Assignments:_____

_____

_____

_____

_____

_____

_____

_____

"Every stumble is not a fall, and every fall does not mean failure." ~Oprah Winfrey

Reflections: _____

_____

_____

_____

_____

_____

_____

_____

_____

_____

_____

_____

_____

_____

_____

_____

_____

_____

_____

"Eighty percent of success is showing up." ~Woody Allen

Session Date: _____

Coach: _____ **Time:** _____

Agenda: _____

_____

_____

_____

_____

Aha Moment: _____

_____

_____

_____

Assignments: _____

_____

_____

_____

_____

_____

_____

_____

*"When your dream is bigger than you are, you only have
two choices: give up or get help." ~John C. Maxwell*

Reflections: _____

_____

_____

_____

_____

_____

_____

_____

_____

_____

_____

_____

_____

_____

_____

_____

_____

_____

_____

_____

_____

"The difference between a successful person and others is not a lack of strength, not a lack of knowledge, but rather a lack of will." ~**Vince Lombardi**

Session Date: _____

Coach: _____ **Time:** _____

Agenda: _____

_____

_____

_____

_____

Aha Moment: _____

_____

_____

_____

Assignments:_____

_____

_____

_____

_____

_____

_____

_____

_____

"I think how you start the day many times determines what kind of day you're going to have." ~Joel Osteen

Reflections: _____

_____

_____

_____

_____

_____

_____

_____

_____

_____

_____

_____

_____

_____

_____

_____

_____

_____

"If what you are doing is not moving you towards your goals, then it's moving you away from your goals."
~Brian Tracy

Session Date: _____

Coach: _____**Time:** _____

Agenda: _____

_____

_____

_____

_____

Aha Moment: _____

_____

_____

_____

Assignments:_____

_____

_____

_____

_____

_____

_____

_____

_____

"When it is obvious that the goals cannot be reached, don't adjust the goals, adjust the action steps." ~Confucius

Reflections: _____

_____

_____

_____

_____

_____

_____

_____

_____

_____

_____

_____

_____

_____

_____

_____

_____

_____

"Kindness is the language which the deaf can hear and the blind can see." ~Mark Twain

Session Date: _____

Coach: _____ **Time:** _____

Agenda: _____

_____

_____

_____

_____

Aha Moment: _____

_____

_____

_____

Assignments: _____

_____

_____

_____

_____

_____

_____

_____

"If opportunity doesn't knock, build a door." ~**Milton Berle**

Reflections: _____

"Your attitude, not your aptitude, will determine your altitude." ~Zig Ziglar

Session Date: _____

Coach: _____ **Time:** _____

Agenda: _____

_____

_____

_____

_____

Aha Moment: _____

_____

_____

_____

Assignments: _____

_____

_____

_____

_____

_____

_____

_____

"I've learned that you shouldn't go through life with a catcher's mitt on both hands; you need to be able to throw something back." ~Maya Angelou

Reflections: _____

_____

_____

_____

_____

_____

_____

_____

_____

_____

_____

_____

_____

_____

_____

_____

_____

_____

_____

_____

_____

"Our greatest glory is not in never falling, but in rising every time we fall." ~Confucius

Session Date: _____

Coach: _____ **Time:** _____

Agenda: _____

_____

_____

_____

_____

Aha Moment: _____

_____

_____

_____

Assignments: _____

_____

_____

_____

_____

_____

_____

"The secret of your success is determined by your daily agenda." ~John C. Maxwell

Reflections: _____

_____

_____

_____

_____

_____

_____

_____

_____

_____

_____

_____

_____

_____

_____

_____

_____

_____

"Nobody made a greater mistake than he who did nothing because he could do only a little." ~Edmund Burke

Session Date: _____

Coach: _____**Time:** _____

Agenda: _____

_____

_____

_____

_____

Aha Moment: _____

_____

_____

_____

Assignments:_____

_____

_____

_____

_____

_____

_____

_____

*"Blessed are those who hunger and thirst for righteousness, for they shall be satisfied." ~**Matthew 5:11***

Reflections: _____

_____

_____

_____

_____

_____

_____

_____

_____

_____

_____

_____

_____

_____

_____

_____

_____

_____

_____

_____

"You cannot have a positive life and a negative mind."
~Joyce Meyer

Session Date: _____

Coach: _____ **Time:** _____

Agenda: _____

_____

_____

_____

_____

Aha Moment: _____

_____

_____

_____

Assignments: _____

_____

_____

_____

_____

_____

_____

_____

"Your imagination is your preview of life's coming attractions." ~Albert Einstein

Reflections: _____

_____

_____

_____

_____

_____

_____

_____

_____

_____

_____

_____

_____

_____

_____

_____

_____

_____

_____

"Life isn't about finding yourself. Life is about creating yourself." ~George Bernard Shaw

Session Date: _____

Coach: _____ **Time:** _____

Agenda: _____

_____

_____

_____

_____

Aha Moment: _____

_____

_____

_____

Assignments: _____

_____

_____

_____

_____

_____

_____

_____

"There's an important difference between giving up and letting go." ~Jessica Hatchigan

Reflections: _____

_____

_____

_____

_____

_____

_____

_____

_____

_____

_____

_____

_____

_____

_____

_____

_____

_____

"Most people have never learned that one of the main aims in life is to enjoy it." ~**Samuel Butler**

Session Date: _____

Coach: _____ **Time:** _____

Agenda: _____

_____

_____

_____

_____

Aha Moment: _____

_____

_____

_____

Assignments: _____

_____

_____

_____

_____

_____

_____

_____

"Call those things that be not as though they were."
~Romans 4:17 NIV

Reflections: _____

_____

_____

_____

_____

_____

_____

_____

_____

_____

_____

_____

_____

_____

_____

_____

_____

_____

_____

"The best way to predict the future is to create it."
~Peter Drucker

Session Date: _____

Coach: _____**Time:** _____

Agenda: _____

_____

_____

_____

_____

Aha Moment: _____

_____

_____

_____

Assignments:_____

_____

_____

_____

_____

_____

_____

_____

"We are what we repeatedly do. Excellence, then, is not an act, but a habit." ~Aristotle

Reflections: _____

_____

_____

_____

_____

_____

_____

_____

_____

_____

_____

_____

_____

_____

_____

_____

_____

_____

"One of the best things to do sometimes is simply to be."
~Eric Butterworth

Session Date: _____

Coach: _____**Time:** _____

Agenda: _____

_____

_____

_____

_____

Aha Moment: _____

_____

_____

_____

Assignments:_____

_____

_____

_____

_____

_____

_____

_____

"Vision without action is a daydream. Action without vision is a nightmare." ~Japanese Proverb

Reflections: _____

_____

_____

_____

_____

_____

_____

_____

_____

_____

_____

_____

_____

_____

_____

_____

_____

_____

_____

_____

"An investment in knowledge pays the best interest."
~Benjamin Franklin

Session Date: _____

Coach: _____**Time:** _____

Agenda: _____

_____

_____

_____

_____

Aha Moment: _____

_____

_____

_____

Assignments:_____

_____

_____

_____

_____

_____

_____

_____

"Don't ask what the world needs. Ask what makes you come alive, and go do it. Because what the world needs is people who have come alive." ~Howard Thurman

Reflections: _____

_____

_____

_____

_____

_____

_____

_____

_____

_____

_____

_____

_____

_____

_____

_____

_____

_____

"If life had a second edition, how would you re-write the script?" ~Tina Frizzell-Jenkins

Session Date: _____

Coach: _____ **Time:** _____

Agenda: _____

_____

_____

_____

_____

Aha Moment: _____

_____

_____

_____

Assignments: _____

_____

_____

_____

_____

_____

_____

_____

"If you want to find God, hang out in the space between your thoughts." ~Alan Cohen

Reflections: _____

_____

_____

_____

_____

_____

_____

_____

_____

_____

_____

_____

_____

_____

_____

_____

_____

_____

_____

"Rarely do we find men who willingly engage in hard, solid thinking. There is an almost universal quest for easy answers and half-baked solutions. Nothing pains some people more than having to think."
~Martin Luther King, Jr.

Session Date: _____

Coach: _____**Time:** _____

Agenda: _____

_____

_____

_____

_____

Aha Moment: _____

_____

_____

_____

Assignments:_____

_____

_____

_____

_____

_____

_____

_____

"Reduce your plan to writing. The moment you complete this, you will have definitely given concrete form to the intangible desire." ~Napoleon Hill

Reflections: _____

_____

_____

_____

_____

_____

_____

_____

_____

_____

_____

_____

_____

_____

_____

_____

_____

_____

"You grow up the day you have your first real laugh—at yourself" **~Ethel Barrymore**

Session Date: _____

Coach: _____ **Time:** _____

Agenda: _____

_____

_____

_____

_____

Aha Moment: _____

_____

_____

_____

Assignments: _____

_____

_____

_____

_____

_____

_____

_____

"If you can find a path with no obstacles, it probably doesn't lead anywhere." ~**Frank Clark**

Reflections: _____

_____

_____

_____

_____

_____

_____

_____

_____

_____

_____

_____

_____

_____

_____

_____

_____

"Happiness is not something you postpone for the future; it is something you design for the present." ~**Jim Rohn**

Session Date: _____

Coach: _____**Time:** _____

Agenda: _____

_____

_____

_____

_____

Aha Moment: _____

_____

_____

_____

Assignments:_____

_____

_____

_____

_____

_____

_____

_____

"The best things in life are not things." ~**Unknown**

Reflections: _____

_____

_____

_____

_____

_____

_____

_____

_____

_____

_____

_____

_____

_____

_____

_____

_____

_____

_____

"You can change your world by changing your words...
Remember, death and life are in the power of the tongue."
~Joel Osteen

Journaling Ends

Creator of the
Read Up Jot Down Series

Tina Frizzell-Jenkins
a.k.a.
Coach Tina FJ
www.readupjotdownjournal.com
www.coachtinafj.com
or
CoachTinaFJ@tinafrizzell.com

Resources

To get a copy of these resources
and many others,
visit coachtinafj.com today!

www.ingramcontent.com/pod-product-compliance
Lightning Source LLC
Chambersburg PA
CBHW072156090426
42740CB00012B/2291